THE WORD IS...

THE
WORD IS...

Ralph Rhea

HAWTHORN BOOKS, INC.
W. Clement Stone, Publisher
NEW YORK

Contents

THE WORD IS...

THE WORD IS
Ability

When thinking of abilities that we want to develop, we should include the ability to handle problem situations as they arise. Just as many people have a low pain threshold, many may also have a low threshold for disappointment, sorrow, irritation, or anxiety. Meeting these feelings through some form of escape or developing indifference demands too high a price. We all have the innate ability, when developed, that enables us to meet each day's problems with poise and each unexpected crisis with strength and courage.

THE WORD IS
Absolute

Quite often we cause difficulties for ourselves by trying to make relative things absolute. No person we know is absolutely the same all the time. No life situation is absolutely permanent and inevitable. No absolute future can be determined. It is helpful to keep in mind that relative conditions are relative and can be changed. Nothing has happened in your life in the past that can be changed. Nothing has happened in your life in the past that can't be transcended by what you do today or tomorrow. The door is always open for change and improvement.

THE WORD IS
Accept

Our relations with others improve rapidly as we learn to accept people as they are. We may often fail to fully accept the very ones we love most because we hold high ideals for them and will accept nothing less. It is quite conceivable to see great possibilities for achievement and growth in some person, but at the same time accept him where he is now. We need to remember that idealism without flexibility stifles, but linked with acceptance it may help someone express his highest self.

THE WORD IS
Acceptance

To be fully accepted by everyone is probably an unattainable goal; however, it is a wonderful feeling when there is someone with whom we can discuss our inmost, honest feelings and know that we are accepted. It is also a milestone in our life when we can learn to accept ourselves. There always seems to be a gap between what we are and what we would like to be. We should be like Noah in the beautiful play *Green Pastures* when he said, "I ain't much, but I'se all I got."

THE WORD IS
Accomplishment

In the field of all human endeavor one fact stands out above all others. If we truly desire to accomplish something, we must gather the resources to form an image of ourselves as being completely capable of reaching what we want to accomplish. We observe in ourselves or others that the goal may be practical, positive, and easily within our reach, but we have an image of ourselves as something less than capable. There is no magic formula, but when you turn your mind toward gaining a good self-image, the results may seem like magic to you!

THE WORD IS
Achievement

A task performed, a position attained, recognition for performance, or earning a certain amount of money may all be looked upon as achievement. As long as this is the only measuring stick, we may be putting ourselves into the land of "never enough." True achievement almost has to become something very subjective inside ourselves where we feel achievement even though others may not recognize it. To have the inner sense of achievement is better than world recognition.

THE WORD IS
Action

If someone asked you what kind of a day you were going to have, would you answer, "I don't know. I will have to wait and see how other people act." This attitude causes us to give other people the power to make or break the day for us. What we really are saying is that we have no course of action but to wait until some reaction sets in. To go through a whole day simply reacting is to live without plan or purpose for that day. When a course of action is clearly set forth, we cooperate but we do not just spend our day reacting.

THE WORD IS
Adjustment

This word should not be confused with passivity or quiet repression of one's true feelings. Quite often the "well-adjusted" husband leaves home and is never heard from again, or the "well-adjusted" wife buries her disappointment and frustrations, but very seldom expresses her true feelings. This is not to say that we can always express everything we feel, but complete suppression or seeking a means of escape is not the answer. We have to make adjustments to life and living every day, but completely giving up the freedom to express one's natural feelings is too high a price to pay for being "well-adjusted."

THE WORD IS
Adventure

This very word is considered by some to be rhetorical and without much meaning. Don't believe it. The greatest adventure lies not in some far-off place but in yourself. A mountain climber begins by asking, "How high is the peak? What is the best way to start? What supplies will I need in order to reach the summit?" Exploring the inner life causes us to ask, "What caused me to be like I am? How can I better understand myself? What resources do I have to help me?" This can become the most exciting adventure that life has to offer.

THE WORD IS
Affirmation

To find contentment in the heart and a sense of fulfillment in the mind, we must learn to affirm life and the goodness of living. Not by hating others, but by loving them; not by harming, but by helping; not by despairing, but by hoping do we find the strength and courage to give to life and take from life. It is not even the final goal that is important, but rather the journey. There will always be that which will tempt you to deny the worthwhileness of life, but affirmation is always more powerful than denial.

THE WORD IS
Alone

Some people speak of being alone as if it implies some kind of threat that should be avoided at all cost. But you know, there are some circumstances in our lives that can be handled properly only after a time of solitude. It is when we draw apart from a busy world and seek new sources of inspiration that, from somewhere deep inside our own being, the voice of creative imagination speaks and the answers to our problems come with great clarity. Being alone need not be loneliness.

THE WORD IS
Ambivalence

This is a word used by many, who often have only a vague knowledge of what it means. As simply put as possible, it means to have thoughts, deep feelings, or desires that appear to oppose one another. For instance, we want to belong to a family, to a group, or to other people, but at the same time we want to keep our own identities or individuality. The reason is that both feelings relate to a basic need and are not as opposite as they may seem. If you have "ambivalent" feelings or desires, put them together. Make them work with and for each other and you'll be a stronger person for it.

THE WORD IS
Amiable

It is scarcely possible to overestimate the gains that come to any individual who learns to be amiable. People trust him because they are sure they will not become the object of some sudden outburst of anger. They enjoy him because he is not subject to rapidly changing moods. Being open, kind, and good-natured most of the time requires discipline and practice, but it pays high dividends.

THE WORD IS
Answer

New situations that arise in government, politics, our society, or our personal lives force us to try to find satisfactory answers. It is then that we discover living is somewhat like a jigsaw puzzle. We read the newspapers, watch television, listen to varied opinions, and try to put things together piece by piece. But it is through our own perceptual powers that we find answers. They may not be final and complete, but they are answers and they serve the purpose of dissolving doubt and confusion.

THE WORD IS
Anticipation

The person who anticipates the very best may be called foolish, unrealistic, or overly optimistic. But this is far better than falling into the trap of anticipating the very worst. It does seem at times that those who anticipate the worst get it. Quite often a person who anticipates the best is prepared to link that with the ability to make something good out of whatever comes his way. This is an unbeatable formula. Never let the yesterday's disappointments rob you of the ability to feel joyous anticipation for all the tomorrows to come!

THE WORD IS
Appearances

It is truly a fact of life that we cannot judge by appearances. When we have moments of discouragement, we are sometimes prone to judge ourselves and others as selfish, thoughtless, or self-centered. We have reason to think this when we judge only by appearances. We all know that there is that in us that longs to be loved and accepted. We also know that we long to be more loving and that we actually possess the capacity to express these desires in the right way. Appearances are often poor guides for passing judgment.

THE WORD IS
Application

Most of us read many books, listen to lectures, and sometimes study for long hours. But the knowledge we gather in these ways is of little value to us until we apply it. There is the story of an agriculturist who was trying to sell a farmer an expensive book and he said, "This book will teach you how to farm a lot better." Back came the honest answer, "Oh, no thanks, I ain't farmin' as good as I know how already!" Well, friends, we all know that very few days are filled with learning something entirely new, but happy is the day when something inspires us to apply what we already know.

THE WORD IS
Appreciation

A person who never gives any thought about expressing appreciation to others has become self-centered. However, there are many of us who would like to express appreciation but are reluctant to do so, thinking it might be misunderstood. Very few people like to flatter or be flattered, but we all like appreciation. The only way to overcome our reluctance is to consciously and deliberately practice it every day. Observing how a little appreciation lights up a person's life quickly develops the urge to express it more often.

THE WORD IS
Art

The most important art form that we know about is the art of living. Two people may be employed in a job where their duties are identical. One seems nervous, tense, and very much in a hurry. The other may be relaxed, easygoing, and apparently enjoying what he is doing. If you saw the same two playing bridge, golf, conversing, or whatever, it would be apparent that one was practicing the art of living and the other was not. Do you try too hard, get overly anxious, or build tension? If you do, join the club. But remember, you have as much talent for learning and practicing the art of living as anyone else.

THE WORD IS
Assurance

One of the greatest attributes we can develop is a strong feeling of assurance. This means having the assurance that if something is wrong, it can be made right; if we are down, we can get up again; if conditions are bad, they can be improved. Out of confusion will come a feeling of direction. If there is a gap between our ideals, aspirations, and desires, compared to the way we are living our lives, the gap can be closed. The feeling of assurance must be sought, cultivated, and expressed. It is attainable and within our grasp, but we have to reach for it constantly.

THE WORD IS
Atonement

We can overlook an important factor in our life if we feel that atonement should be thought of exclusively in terms of theology. We all have a need for atonement. Even the slightest act that violates our conscience may cause guilt feelings that cannot be ignored. Far too many people carry a burden of irrational guilt that is all out of proportion to any wrong that was committed. Forgive yourself! Let go of the past. Make what amends you can and do the best you can in the present. This is atonement, too.

THE WORD IS
Attention

The basic need for love and attention is present all through our life. Sometimes we are ashamed of this need and will not give it conscious recognition, but this does not cause it to go away. To feel the need for love and attention but refuse to admit it only causes us to engage in blaming others. Employer, children, husband, or wife can become the object of our grievances. It is much easier to recognize our need and prepare to receive it when it comes our way.

THE WORD IS
Attitude

A friend of mine recently gave me a real lesson in the value of right attitudes. She had remarked she was not feeling too well, and I asked, "Do you have to go to work tomorrow?" Without hesitation she replied, "I like to go to work." Whether or not she just natually liked her work or had learned to like it is beside the point. I had the feeling that it made her feel better just thinking about her work. It was a strong reminder of how, on any given day, so very much depends on right attitudes!

THE WORD IS
Author

We are all authors—writing something each day in the book of our own life. Whatever your age, don't fall into the trap of writing your conclusion. In the years past you have only written the prologue. Now you are ready for the real story. There is precious time left for you to write from the wisdom you have gained. There is time to write of interest and excitement and joyous experiences beyond your fondest expectations. You may not set it down in words, but what you live and think and experience makes you the author of your life and it does not need a conclusion.

THE WORD IS
Awaken

Every one of us has talents, powers, and abilities that he has not yet awakened. We seem to treat them like a sleeping child and say, "Do not disturb—he needs his rest." Meanwhile, we struggle and strive to find answers to new problems by using the same old methods. "Why is this? Why do we disregard the unique gifts and talents that we may possess?" Perhaps we are afraid that if we awaken them, they will push us to do different things. And this is true. They will push, but always towards something better.

THE WORD IS
Balance

To live the balanced life is to live the good life. We can be too placid or too aggressive, work too hard or too little, be too concerned or not concerned enough. Even in nature we observe the laws of checks and balances. Whoever first said that "all things should be done in moderation" hit upon a great truth. It is quite possible to have "too much of a good thing." If we remain aware of this law of balance, we will take better care of our minds, bodies, and affairs and, by doing so, improve the quality of our life.

THE WORD IS
Beauty

To say that "beauty is in the eye of the beholder" is almost an understatement. Quite often natural beauty around us is lavish. However, it is possible for us to be caught up in the complexities of life until we may not really see it. If nature could speak, we might be told to look around and behold the beauty of each flower and tree, and of every growing thing. If you fail to see them, they are not there. Perhaps this is also true of people. The beauty is there if you will behold it.

THE WORD IS
Becoming

Our whole life is spent in a state of becoming. It is strange to hear people say that human nature never changes, when it is the one kind of nature that does change. Physically, mentally, emotionally, we are never quite the same from day to day or week to week. Yet there appears to be a strong tendency to place limitations on ourselves and others. I am me and you are you and there is nothing either of us can do about it. But there is something we can do. We can remember that we are in a state of becoming and can even choose the direction towards that which we wish to become.

THE WORD IS
Beginning

It has always been inspiring to me to think of each day as a new beginning. If you have come to the end of one era of your life, you have a choice. You can let the curtain down and say, "The end," or you can raise the curtain and begin the second act. You can use your experience as a springboard to new and better things. If you listen closely to life, it may be saying, "Go ahead, pitch in, fire away, take off! Today is a new beginning!"

THE WORD IS
Behold

I remember, at one time, when I was going through a sad experience, I had such a strong feeling that it would never pass and that unhappiness would remain with me forever. But I was wrong. There came a time when I felt like shouting to the world, "Behold! It has passed and, through it, I have learned to enjoy life more deeply than before!" And that's the way life is. In the words of Whittier, "The night is mother of the day, the winter of the spring."

THE WORD IS
Being

When we listen to people discussing the theories of art, literature, music, religion, or whatever, it is easy to get the impression that many think talking about something is really the same as real accomplishment in any field. The reality of life is being and doing. Our values, ideals, and whole philosophy of life are revealed in what we are. If we want to tell the world what our real values are, we are required to live, act, react, and become that which we would like to be.

THE WORD IS
Birth

If you take a close look at your life span, you can quickly get the feeling that you have, in fact, lived several lives in this one lifetime. That is the way it should be, but the difficulty arises if we try to cling to a part of life that no longer exists. Living, growing, and maturing requires that we be ready and willing to accept new birth. There can be the birth of new concepts about ourselves and life in general; higher vision, deeper satisfaction, and greater creative potential can be born in us when we remove barriers of the past.

27

THE WORD IS
Breakthrough

To say that our whole life is programmed by the combination of inheritance through genes is less than a half truth. We mostly are what we are because of the way we reacted to life experiences in the past and the way we continue to react in the present. The great breakthrough is possible at any given time. Our whole life can be changed by understanding that inherited factors get weaker and weaker as our positive reactions to life get stronger and stronger. The choice is *yours*, make the breakthrough and the past cannot bind you!

THE WORD IS
Building

We never just live or exist, we are always building. The cornerstone is laid when we are very young, and the building process goes on. It can be routine and monotonous, but we cannot stop the process. A man asked two busy bricklayers what they were doing. One said with some irritation that he was laying bricks. The other stopped, looked up, and answered, "I'm helping to build a building." Who are you—bricklayer or builder?

THE WORD IS
Busy

If you are keeping busy at many different activities, don't forget to keep busy at enjoying life. This not only means doing things you enjoy, but learning to enjoy whatever you are doing. Two people may be doing the same kind of work, attending the same social events, or taking walks together. One is bored, tired of it all, or thinks something else would be more fun. The other may work with enjoyment in whatever he does. What's the difference? Well, one has learned to keep busy at enjoying life; the other is busy finding reasons not to. Which are you doing?

THE WORD IS
Can

It may seem like a platitude to say that you can accomplish whatever you really want to accomplish. But platitude or not, it is obvious that the words, "I can't," are the most futile, impotent words we can use and often are completely false. Of course, we need to weigh our desires carefully and not try to reach too far, too high, too fast. But make sure that you don't apply the defeatist term of "I can't" to circumstances that should be met with the attitude of "I not only *can*, but I *will!*"

THE WORD IS
Capable

Most of us are capable of performing on a much higher
level than we are on now. Why don't we do so? Well,
undoubtedly, it may be due to our tendency to judge our
capabilities below what they really are. We may feel that
we are making a good effort, but in reality we are working
under a heavy burden of limitations we have set for ourselves. Whatever the reason, if we concentrate on what we
can do instead of giving our attention to our limitations,
we will see ourselves thoroughly capable of moving into a
whole new field of accomplishment.

THE WORD IS
Capacity

Developing our personal capacity for achievement is hard
work, but also can be enjoyable. In whatever we are doing,
the hard work comes easier when we learn to enjoy the on-
going process and the net results. It is difficult to think of
anything that brings more real satisfaction than developing some skill or using some potential capacity to a much
higher degree than we have in the past.

THE WORD IS
Care

Everyone has a basic need for knowing that no matter what happens in our life, someone cares. The "silent scream" is often caused by a person suffering inside himself and feeling that no one cares. Today, let's all make it our goal to let someone know we care. Often a person may be lifted right out of a depressed state by knowing that someone cares. Stop and think! It is almost awe-inspiring to know that we have such a power but may live through a day without using it.

THE WORD IS
Caring

In the beautifully written book *Peace of Mind* by Joshua Liebman, a whole chapter is devoted to the subject of "loving one's self properly." This bears no reference to any type of narcissism, but rather to the simple process of caring. How much do you care for your body, your mind, your thoughts, your feelings, and all that is you? It is almost automatic that when there is a proper caring for one's self, there comes a greater caring for others.

THE WORD IS
Castle

Has someone scoffed at you for building a "castle in the air"? Don't tear it down on that account. Make it real. Every invention, every achievement, every "castle" has to exist in the air at first. It is born as an idea, just an airy figment of the brain. Never give up an idea just because other people don't think much of it. Thoreau said: "If you have built castles in the air, your work need not be lost; that is where they should be. Now put the foundations under them."

THE WORD IS
Cause

From the simplest to the most complicated difficulties in life, the cause must be found before the situation improves. Most of the time we deal with symptoms, not causes. A person describes how he "feels" in terms of symptoms. The social conditions we see are symptoms. Inharmony in relations with others is a symptom. We should begin to ask, "I know what I see and feel, but what is the *cause?*" A search for the cause impels one to deal in depth with what bothers him most.

THE WORD IS
Center

A large body of evidence could be compiled to show that we all have a center or a core of wisdom and guidance in our consciousness that can be relied upon totally. The only catch is that we lose touch with it through constantly seeking guidance outside ourselves. In regard to the values an individual lives by, outside advice can be confusing or totally wrong. The task is to get back in touch with the center of your being for whatever guidance you need. If what you receive lessens confusion, promises greater fulfillment for yourself and others, and makes you feel good, you can be confident that you have touched the right place.

THE WORD IS
Change

Everyone in the public eye knows that it is possible to be a hero one day and the next a villain. But even more touching is the person unprepared to meet the changes that come slowly but surely in any field of endeavor. Arthur Miller, in his play, *Death of a Salesman*, has the wife of Willie Loman saying, "He's a man way out there in the blue, riding on a smile and a shoeshine. And when they start not smiling back, that's an earthquake." Change is exhilarating or fearsome, depending on whether or not we are ready.

THE WORD IS
Channel

Think of yourself as an open channel through which life, energy, and vitality flow. We did not invent those qualities nor do we by ourselves sustain them. Trees, flowers, grass, and other growing things take different substances into their roots from sunlight, air, and water and convert them into the oxygen that we breathe. Similarly, we exhale carbon dioxide, which is absorbed, purified, and returned to us in the form of oxygen. The more we think of ourselves as open channels for life, the more vital and energetic we become.

THE WORD IS
Cheerful

Everyone loves to be around a cheerful person because he seems to change and lift up the attitudes of everyone around him. If you don't consider yourself a cheerful person, try a little experiment. When you awaken in the morning, say to yourself, "Today I am going to be as cheerful as possible!" Then make that one of your projects for the day. This has deeper meaning than some might believe. Cheerfulness can help you handle any situation with far more effectiveness.

THE WORD IS
Comparison

When we think about the accomplishments of others or read about some outstanding person, we may be prone to start the negative process of making ourselves "suffer by comparison." How often do you hear someone say, "Other people accomplish goals that I would like to reach, but let's face it, I don't have the talent, imagination, or ability." If you are going to make comparisons, why not give yourself a break and adopt the attitude of the poet who wrote: "I do not envy anyone, nor the place he has carved for himself in the sun. I have dreams to dream, and work to do, and there's room in the sun for us all to walk through."

THE WORD IS
Compensation

Most of what is really worthwhile in life comes to us as compensation for working to attain it. Such is the case with happiness and real satisfaction. When we are unhappy, we must find out why and work to overcome the unhappy state. We are required to find out what really makes us happy and be willing to work constantly to attain and maintain the state of happiness. When we fully understand that this is a lifetime task, we will continue to work at it and our compensation will be assured.

THE WORD IS
Competent

No one can deny the fact that we live in a rapidly changing world, and we need increasing competence for living life and meeting these changes. This comes to us by eradicating obsolete and outgrown ideas. We cannot meet the present if we carry a burden of guilt about the past. The mind needs occasional renovating to sweep out the cobwebs of unnecessary limitation. This means work, but it brings increased competence for living life and facing the present and future with a sense of joy.

THE WORD IS
Competition

To some, this may seem like a hard word in the highly competitive society in which we live. However, there can be a wholesome, positive approach to competition. We can compete with our past performance. In any task at hand, we can be a good competitor, which means that we are willing to give our concentration and diligence to whatever we are doing. In other words, we are making the all-out effort to perform at a higher level than ever before. The best kind of competition is to forget others and to express our own talents and abilities.

THE WORD IS
Compromise

This word has many different meanings, but let's consider the times when it is an advantage to be willing to compromise. Have you ever known a person who was truly stubborn and rigid and refused to change his mind, regardless of evidence that he was wrong? Compare this to the one who is willing to compromise, the one who says, "I have strong opinions about this, but I am willing to listen. Perhaps I could be wrong." Nothing is gained by building a wall around our opinions, through which no new viewpoint can either come in or go out.

THE WORD IS
Concentration

If we attempted to draw a picture of a person deep in concentration, he would probably have a furrowed brow, look anything but cheerful, and might even show some signs of anxiety. But concentration can be much more than that. Have you ever experienced a time when it seemed that all your faculties were working together? Your thoughts, your feelings, your desires, and attitudes were all in harmony? When in quiet contemplation you achieve this feeling, there also will come the assurance that all things are working together for your good.

THE WORD IS
Condition

It seems a little fearsome to go against the opinions expressed by so many eminent authors on the subject of the human condition and human conditioning, but I have never been able to accept total conditioning as a life concept. We are told that by the time we are five, seven, ten, or twenty years old we have been so conditioned that our whole life pattern is set. Of course we are conditioned, but never totally. Inheritance and early environment are not as important as what you do with them. Remember that you have the power to change and to overcome.

THE WORD IS
Conflict

Living with others and working with others is to invite conflict. And what shall we do when conflict comes? Run away, fight, become defensive? There is an art of using conflict in a constructive way. As in any other art it is not come by easily. We must be willing to ask ourselves some honest questions. Why the disagreement? Why the conflict? Am I open to the views of those around me? It is difficult to believe that a deeper concern for other's feelings and a higher degree of accomplishment can come out of conflict, but it happens constantly for those who have learned the art.

THE WORD IS
Consistent

However excellent some idea may be in regard to improving the quality of our life, it is of no real value until it is consistently applied. You may find it helpful to keep a written record. Take any quality you wish to express in your life and write your thoughts, desires, and intentions in a record book. Keep the record handy so you can make new entries. You will easily see whether or not you are being consistent. The best of intentions must be strengthened by consistent application.

THE WORD IS
Conviction

One of the most valuable goals we can have is to establish and maintain the conviction that things have a way of working out and that good will manifest itself. This is especially true in the midst of confused times. After all the long discussions and various opinions about the government, politics, the state of our economy, or some intensely personal problem, what holds you steady, lifts you above confusion and doubt and gives you comfort? Is it not the conviction that you can weather the storm because you are in charge of your life?

THE WORD IS
Courage

Meeting our life situations in a way that brings right results always demands the quality of courage. Sometimes this may even mean the courage to fail. We can learn as much from failure as from success. If you have a deep desire to do something, do it. Then remember that, if it fails, it does not mean that you are a failure. It really means you had the courage to try.

THE WORD IS
Decision

A friend of mine said, "My life would have been much better if I had learned a long time ago how to make decisions!" He was not complaining about his inability to make decisions, but rather that the decisions he made had so often been wrong. A good way to sharpen our decisive powers is to put our decisions in terms of "yes" and "no." Many times, when we say "yes" to something, we are saying "no" to something else. We need a clear understanding of what we are saying "yes" to and what we are saying "no" to. Right decisions require clear thinking.

THE WORD IS
Defenses

We all build defenses against the threats of life, whether real or imagined. Unfortunately, the cure is sometimes as bad as the disease. When others hurt, humiliate, or express antagonism toward us, we react according to our defenses, some of which are to escape, withdraw, avoid, or react in turn by open hostility. There are better ways. Build your self-confidence. Learn to feel good about yourself. Find a basis for understanding the feelings and actions of others. It will do you no harm and is certain to help your relationships with others.

THE WORD IS
Delight

Some words serve as a guide to discovering whether or not we are really enjoying life. Such a word is delight. It carries the meaning of extreme satisfaction, gratification, or joy. How many things have you done in the last week or month that brought you great delight and that you really enjoyed doing? If you cannot think of any or perhaps of only a few moments of great enjoyment, you may have to relearn the habit of delighting in what you are doing or to begin to seek out that which does bring you delight.

THE WORD IS
Dialogue

Quite often that which we call dialogue with another person is more like verbal fencing. We must parry the thrust, keep our defenses up, move with quick wit to give thrust for thrust. How wonderful it is to engage in dialogue with another that consists of sincerity, good humor, trust, and a sense of caring. Remember that there are people all around you who long for such an exchange. You will find deep satisfaction in establishing yourself as a person who keeps confidences and can accept another for what he is without passing judgment.

THE WORD IS
Different

It seems to take a long time to learn the important lesson that tells us each person is different and must be treated in a manner different from all others. You will find your human relationships deeper and more meaningful if you follow a few simple steps. Give yourself fully to the situation. Free your mind from stereotype methods of working with others. Be conscious of calling forth all your resources in perceiving each person's need and in helping him to fulfill it. Try it, and you'll see it works.

THE WORD IS
Dimension

We all have a past, a present, and a future; we live, move, and have our being in all three. The past may yield pleasant, nostalgic memories, or painful, bitter ones. Past mistakes can best be handled by saying: "It was a learning process and I now put my mistakes where they belong—in the past. It is the present and the future that are magical. I live! I am alive! I have life and energy with which to help myself and to help others who may need me. I am building a positive future by living today in a new dimension of inspiration and love!"

THE WORD IS
Direction

As long as we are moving in some definite direction, we function with a much higher degree of efficiency. No matter what the age of a person, he may come into some situation that seems confusing. We may have some clear aspirations, but never quite seem to live up to them. This may be a chronic feeling, or it can become quite drastic. Whatever the case, we have to find direction. We should decide what courses of action make the most sense to us and then follow them.

THE WORD IS
Dissolve

Do you sometimes feel that your life is a continuing process of problem solving? Even when you find the solution to one problem, another presents itself. In the field of human dynamics, it is often more important to find the cause than to solve each problem separately. It is true that we are often our own worst enemies. If you have any ideal or goal you wish to achieve, look carefully to see if you are throwing up your own roadblock. Your shortcut to success is to dissolve self-defeat!

THE WORD IS
Drive

If you feel that you need more drive to accomplish your goals, be sure you make the distinction between drive and driven. A person who is driven usually makes quite a fuss about how much work he has to do and what long hours he puts in. He may be trying to do that which others think he ought to do. He may be trying to achieve someone else's definition of success. You will find the drive you need when you quietly decide on the goals you wish to achieve and confidently move towards achieving them.

THE WORD IS
Effort

At the pace our world is moving, it sometimes seems to take a tremendous effort to stay even. It becomes increasingly important that the effort we do put forth each day is channeled in the right directions. Without overall life goals as well as short-term objectives, it is easy to waste time, waste effort, and make unwise choices. Time spent in planning our lives, regularly reviewing our plans, and sticking to them, results in maximum mileage for every effort.

THE WORD IS
Emphasis

Have you ever watched two persons go through a similar difficult experience and seen one become disorganized and confused while the other resolutely masters what he faces? We wonder how this can be when both seem to possess a good amount of intelligence. One explanation is that in a time of challenge some people from habit emphasize their inability to meet the challenge; others marshal all their forces for the victory. Emphasis on your strongest attributes is the best assurance of mastery!

THE WORD IS
Encourage

To try to help someone naturally implies that the person has a problem, and all too often we keep our eye on the problem rather than on the person's good potential. If you really want to help in an encouraging way, you must help through a person's strength, not his weakness. One poet says:

> When 'er I try to help a stumbling one,
> Let me be tolerantly silent of the past,
> Let me consider not what he has done,
> But what he may do now.

Help others with this encouraging thought: "I see the best and highest self in you; I see its fullest expression now."

48

THE WORD IS
Environment

When we think of the environment in which we live, our minds automatically turn to conditions around us or outside our own being. The kinds of people with whom we work and live, the quality of the air we breathe, and economic factors are some of the elements that we think of as our environment. It is the way of wisdom to give as much or more attention to our inner environment. How capable am I of giving and receiving love? How do I use inner resources to overcome fear, frustration, or resentment? Creating the right inner environment invariably has a direct effect on all that goes on around us.

THE WORD IS
Exchange

If we take the time to listen to conversations that go on around us, we become highly aware of the importance of a real exchange of ideas. What a delight it is either to listen to or enter into a conversation when a real exchange of thoughts and ideas is taking place. At such a time there is respect for the opinions of others, even though there may not be total agreement. To be willing to exchange ideas is to multiply our knowledge and wisdom.

THE WORD IS
Express

One of the most important and most difficult lessons we have to learn is to allow each person the space and freedom to express himself in his own way. Most of us don't really want to be domineering, but there is a strong tendency to want those around us to think as we think, act as we act, feel as we feel, and to follow our concepts instead of their own. There is such a vast difference in individuals that to try to make others fit into our mold is to fail. Your own sense of freedom is greatly strengthened when you learn to free others to express themselves in their own way.

THE WORD IS
Expression

Much frustration is built up inside ourselves when we do not express our talent in some manner. From the beginning of life we have "input" from family, friends, teachers, and life experiences. To balance this, some people paint, some play music, some write and thus find satisfactory means of expression. You may not think of your talent as being of the stature of genius, but it doesn't have to be. It is important to your happiness and well-being to find the avenue of expression that suits you best and move with courage to express it.

50

THE WORD IS
Flexibility

The tree that is rigid often breaks in a strong wind. The willow tree is flexible. It dances, flows, gives, as if it enjoys the wind. A person who is flexible is not required to change his ideals and values with the changing winds, but rather to be open-minded and willing to give and take and to change his mind when necessary. If you have times when you feel especially tense, remember that flexibility helps you to move through even the stormiest winds of life without breaking.

THE WORD IS
Forceful

More often than not we think of a forceful person as being domineering, aggressive, or hostile. I vividly remember having a man described to me as being forceful. "He will dominate you if he can." When I met him, what I detected was strength, which came from a healthy, self-affirmation. He believed in his ability and in what he was doing, but he was also kind and concerned about my feelings. I learned that nothing but good can come from learning to be constructively forceful.

THE WORD IS
Forgive

In human relations, if we expect to be forgiven when we do something wrong we must also be willing to forgive others if we feel wronged. At one time I would have rejected the statement that "to forgive is to forget." But the more I think about it the more I am inclined to feel that this is true. To bury resentment is not to forgive. Nor is controlling anger real forgiveness. Wouldn't it be wonderful if we could start each day with a clean slate, having put out of our minds the mistakes of others and feeling confident they have done the same toward us? This would be real forgiveness.

THE WORD IS
Forward

Life seems to be so arranged that we cannot stand still. We must either go forward or slip back. Sometimes events may make the present unattractive, almost unbearable—so that looking back becomes more enticing than looking ahead. You won't be turned into a pillar of salt for looking back, as Lot's wife was; but you will lose touch with the warm, rich "Now" world and gain only shadows in return. The past is gone, so look forward—that's where it's happening and nowhere else!

THE WORD IS
Free

There seems to be a trend toward more and more people believing that they are far from being free in any area of their life. Government, family, and employer are sometimes cited as examples of forces outside themselves impinging on their personal freedom. This is a partial truth; true freedom comes through an inner realization and always has. Every day you are free to make choices and decisions, free to formulate your attitudes and responses to life. We live more easily with outer restrictions if we keep the realization of inner freedom.

THE WORD IS
Freedom

We can never taste the joy of real freedom until we understand that it is a quality that has to be worked out within the realm of our own consciousness. We may be fortunate enough to enjoy a great deal of freedom from restrictions outside ourselves, but our inner life is another matter. Resentment that is allowed to build up, feelings of inferiority, and undue anxiety about little things can have a limiting effect. Like many good things, it does not come easily, but if you want to feel freedom, you must learn to free yourself.

THE WORD IS
Friendliness

It is typical of oriental teaching to define a commonplace attribute in both mystical and practical terms. Buddha defined friendliness as "affection unsullied by hope or thought of any reward on earth or in heaven." To express this kind of friendliness on any given day is to make many people feel better, and, though you genuinely expect no reward, a greater feeling of happiness is bound to come your way.

THE WORD IS
Fulfillment

We all have times when the sense of fulfillment in our lives is missing. More often than not, when this lack of fulfillment seems strongest it is due to the way we have reacted to experiences in the past rather than to what we are doing now. However, there is a strong tendency to blame others for causing our unhappy feelings. We say, if other people were different, our lives would be much more fulfilled. This attitude is not only unproductive, it is destructive. Fortunate is the one who can say, "I blame no one for my feelings. It is my responsibility to find fulfillment now."

THE WORD IS
Future

People who lay claim to the ability to foretell the future are called seers, prophets, or clairvoyants. We are all interested in our future, even though we try to live in the present. For the individual, his future can best be foretold by himself. We know, of course, that environmental factors are involved, but it is much more important to understand that our tomorrow will become the child of the thoughts, actions, and feelings we experience today. Definite goals, strong motivations and desires form the pattern of your future.

THE WORD IS
Game

It is obvious that we all play games with ourselves and the subject is serious enough to deserve consideration. The games we play are for the purpose of fulfilling some need, but we don't want to continue a game in which we are always the loser. The most vivid example is the person who plays the game of "poor little old me." A person who engages in self-pity may drive from his life the very thing he'd like to have. Learning games that harm no one and bring positive results to ourselves assures us of sometimes being in the winner's circle.

THE WORD IS
Gifts

It is a strange fact that many refuse to accept the possibility that they have a special gift that can help them make a real contribution to life. If that is your feeling, it is evidence that you are not very well acquainted with yourself. Closer examination may disclose unique "gifts" in your personality and character that can be easily accentuated. We never can assume that only those with talents on a genuis level can make a real contribution to life.

THE WORD IS
Goodness

If I had to list the deepest regrets of my life, I would probably put at the head of the list the fact that it took me so long to identify with the inherent goodness of others. Each person has particular talents and gifts that he can give to the world. He may not always give them. We may not always approve of his conduct, but the sleeping giant of goodness, talent, and ability is there. By looking long enough you will see it and, perhaps then, be able to help him to see it also.

THE WORD IS
Gratitude

Expressing gratitude for the good things that come our way requires imagination and concentration. How many people have gone out of their way to be helpful to you and are perhaps still doing so? How many problems have you faced where there was no obvious answer, but an answer came? How many times have you felt that you were receiving more from life than you really deserved? Such questions remind us of the good that we have received and help us to cultivate an attitude of gratitude.

THE WORD IS
Guidance

The signs of the times point vividly toward the necessity of learning the art of listening for our own inner guidance and then trusting it. With experts and with those who are not so expert, we constantly hear completely opposite views on almost everything. Sometimes when we express an opinion we may feel like pausing and asking ourselves, "I wonder who made up my mind for me?" You can live by your deepest convictions if you listen to others with an open mind, give due consideration, then turn to your own inner guidance for a reliable answer.

THE WORD IS
Habit

That which we practice with satisfaction becomes the foundation for habit. But what about some habit we have that is distasteful to us and that we would like to break? If you examine it closely, you will see that when the habit was formed it brought you some kind of satisfaction. Consciously, it has outworn its usefulness. A closer look will tell you why you formed the habit in the first place. This is the best way to begin setting yourself free from any habit you no longer need or want.

THE WORD IS
Happiness

Our Constitution says that every man is entitled to life, liberty, and the pursuit of happiness. Any person who spends his life running a race that he is bound to lose is really "out of it." This is, however, the case of those who pursue happiness. It never seems to yield to a direct frontal attack. The happiest people are those who are doing what they like to do and doing it in their best possible manner. Happiness is not a goal, it is a by-product. What do you really like to do? What brings you the greatest fulfillment? If these are the things that take up your time you are probably happy.

THE WORD IS
Happy

You know, there's an old Chinese proverb that says, "If I keep a green bough in my heart, the singing bird will come." It means that if you want to be happy and have good things happen to you, you must create your own climate of happiness. It's your own state of mind that will draw happiness to you. Do you doubt it? Express your happiness and people will beat a path to your door. Happiness seeks the happy!

THE WORD IS
Harmony

In a great work of art, a beautiful nature scene, or a delicious chocolate cake, full appreciation can be felt only when we realize that many different ingredients are in harmony with one another and have been selected and perfectly blended. A sense of harmony is a basic, essential part of our well-being. This means learning to look past the dissonant and live in harmony with ourselves, others, and each life situation. The power is ours to select and blend the ingredients that will produce harmonious nourishment for our deepest needs.

THE WORD IS
Harvest

As the years pass, many people begin to act as though they had just swallowed a calendar; they become preoccupied with the evils of growing old. This can be counteracted by a strong sense of optimism. For everyone there should be a time of harvest, when all the invested years bring the dividends of wisdom and happiness, deeper than anything felt in youth. Even the most cynical cannot make a very good case for pessimism. Look for the best life has to offer and reap the harvest that is yours.

THE WORD IS
Hope

Quite often I hear people talking about hope as if it were a weak word, rather meaningless, and misguiding. The truth is that hope is a guiding light, and without it, life is bleak. If we lose hope, it is not because the world and the people in it have abandoned us, but rather because we have abandoned ourselves. A man in a hospital was thought to be unconscious when the doctor and the nurse agreed that his case was hopeless. He opened his eyes and said, "Continue your treatment. I will tell you when I am hopeless."

THE WORD IS
Humor

In these times it does seem that too many people are taking life as such a deadly serious matter that they lose their sense of humor. We are reminded of this when we get satisfaction out of hearing someone give forth a hearty laugh. Those who have lost their sense of humor usually have a feeling of envy for those who still have the ability to laugh, for they know that something valuable has gone out of their lives. This is not to say that all of life is a laughing matter, but maintaining a sense of humor can be of untold value. If you've lost yours, get it back!

THE WORD IS
Idea

Do you know what is the most powerful thing in the world? No, not the bomb! It's an idea. Ideas change the world more than bombs. Almost a century ago Thomas Edison was granted a patent on his new invention, the incandescent light, and the world of the flickering gas jet was finished. No one knew it yet, of course. They thought electric lights were just a novelty, but in the end they were to light the world to a new brightness. Ideas change the world, and your ideas change your personal world.

THE WORD IS
Idealism

Someone said, *"We* must not teach people the way things *should be* but the way things *are."* Most of us started our lives with certain ideals, but then were disillusioned when we found that life is not like that. The pertinent question then becomes, "What shall we do about it?" Shall we give up our ideals and only look at what is called "reality"? It seems that the strongest person is the one who sees life as it is—but then moves on with everything that is in him to fulfill his idealism.

THE WORD IS
Identify

Our emotions and feelings often become highly intermingled. You may be irritable but are not sure why. Guilt, anxiety, and feelings of depression can all be stirred together but are not exactly the recipe for making a good life. When we are angry, we invariably look for something or someone outside ourselves that is calling forth the anger; but we may just be angry with ourselves. Learn to identify your feelings and their cause and you will learn much about yourself and why you react as you do.

THE WORD IS
Identity

In the world of today it seems to become increasingly imperative for each individual to attain a strong sense of identity. Many people unhesitatingly place this need ahead of security or other basic needs. Ways in which this sense of identity is attained vary among individuals, but it seems to come to the person who can truly say, "I have learned to feel a strong awareness of purpose and meaning in my life. In times of work, recreation, socializing with others, or being alone, I know who I am and why I am here."

THE WORD IS
Image

It is difficult to fully realize how much we live our lives by imagery. Going on a trip or even to the shopping center involves several images before we even start. When this imagery is applied to ourselves, it becomes a powerful agent for doing, learning, or becoming. It works in two ways. When we perform well and have a feeling of success, we have a better image of ourselves. When we have a better image of ourselves, we perform better. Do what it takes to attain a good self-image. You not only need it, you probably deserve it!

THE WORD IS
Imagination

Imagination is both practical and creative. Two boys in a small town, both owning bicycles, applied at the same store for a job. One was hired and the other was not. The one who was hired used his imagination and suggested a new type of quick delivery with his bicycle. How do you use your imagination? It is a quality that we possess and can enhance all through life with proper use. Take some particular situation in your life. Look at it imaginatively from all angles. You may be surprised at what you discover.

THE WORD IS
Independence

When you think of individual independence, you are reminded quickly that to attain desirable character traits one must walk a thin line. The healthy child very quickly sees the value of independence. He cannot depend on his parents or anyone else to do everything for him. He must learn to do for himself. Independence does not mean that we must say to all others, "I do not need you. I can get along without you." To be independent is to feel free to follow one's own ideals and aspirations, but to give loving cooperation to others as we all go forward together.

THE WORD IS
Individual

If you find yourself lacking in self-esteem, remember that what the individual does is the important factor. The consciousness of a community, a nation, and the world is made up of individuals. As an individual, if you dislike yourself, you are sure to dislike others and that much is added to the sum total of your dislike. If, as an individual, you have a healthy self-acceptance and make the effort to learn to like and love others, you will be making a tremendous contribution to the whole world.

THE WORD IS
Insight

Every person has problems, but if you keep on having the same kinds of problems, some insight is indicated. Some people can't get along with their coworkers, some have health problems, others are always broke. If you seem to have the same kind of problem continually, look for insight that reveals the cause. Ask yourself, "What am I doing to invite this? How can I change my way of thinking and avoid having to meet the same challenge?" Solve the inner problem and you will stop meeting the outer one; this requires insight.

THE WORD IS
Joy

To even speak of joy and being a joyous person in the face of the many heavy problems in our world may invite the criticism that one is shallow and unrealistic. The truth is that joy can be equated with a zest for living, creative thinking and acting, high goals and the hope of reaching them. This being the case, it would seem that the very best way possible to help ourselves and the world is to cultivate and express as much joy as possible!

THE WORD IS
Judge

To be too ready with judgments is to be an uncomfortable companion. It is also to run the risk of sometimes being unfair. You seldom know enough about another person and his problems to judge him fairly—so why judge at all? Why not simply keep silent and let time judge? As Shakespeare advised: "Give every man thy ear, but few thy voice; take each man's censure, but reserve thy judgment."

THE WORD IS
Justice

Much unhappiness is caused by feelings of having been dealt with unjustly. On any given day we may feel that we are the victims of injustice with our family, friends, co-workers, or people in general. What's more, it may be true. We may be misquoted, have our intentions misinterpreted, or be totally misunderstood. Whether the injustice is real or imagined is not as important as how we deal with it. To remain poised and calm, to know that the truth will come out, to refuse to give too much importance to little injustices prevents unnecessary unhappiness.

THE WORD IS
Kindness

Whatever we are doing or want to do, it takes no more time and energy to be kind than to be unkind. There is never a time when the need for kindness is lacking. It isn't always easy when we are busy, irritated, or in a hurry, but it would be easier if we knew how much it might mean to someone who has a need. Often what some people pass off as humor is outright unkindness and sarcasm. Kindness is to the human heart as water is to one who thirsts.

THE WORD IS
Knowledge

We have all heard the warning that "a little learning is a dangerous thing." However, it may be more dangerous if it causes us to feel that we never have enough knowledge to make a beginning. If you have goals you aspire to reach, it might be well to remember that any knowledge is helpful and you may wish to begin with what you know now and learn as you go along. We have all known people who seemed almost paralyzed from fear of too little knowledge. A little knowledge is better than none, and coupled with diligence, can open many doors.

THE WORD IS
Laughter

No sound is quite so melodious as the laughter of a delighted child. "How long has it been since you have laughed with real mirth?" The problems of the world are so much with us that we may be prone to take everything too seriously. To be sure, living is a serious business, but we must be sure that we do not forget how to laugh. To say that laughter is good medicine is an understatement. Laughter is the best form of relaxation and often serves to restore the right perspective in serious matters.

THE WORD IS
Learn

Most that is worthwhile in life is not something given to us but is something we have learned. We have to learn to give love and receive love. We must learn to meet unexpected circumstances with poise and confidence. We have to learn how to be happy and enjoy life. We have to learn to control our thoughts and attitudes and change them when we do not get the right results. All this can be accomplished when we learn to push our thoughts around instead of letting them push us around.

THE WORD IS
Leisure

We see a strange paradox in people who work hard for many years so that they can retire and have time for leisure and then find the hours resting heavily on their shoulders. Observe children at play and you will often see a powerful truth demonstrated. Real enjoyment of leisure time can come only with a sense of freedom and imagination. Anyone who keeps his imagination alive will never retire to a land of limbo.

THE WORD IS
Liberate

Very few persons think of themselves as being liberated,
mainly because the same unhappy feelings, the same reactions to certain situations, and the same binding attitudes
keep cropping up. A good axiom to remember is: "Nothing
can be solved in the same consciousness from which it was
created in the first place." Since our deepest problems are
within ourselves, that is where we must begin to solve
them. The liberated person is the one who knows that
there are new ways, new ideas, or a whole new way of life
available to him if he continues to search.

THE WORD IS
Liberty

To enjoy the quality of liberty and freedom there are some
areas of our lives to which we must be bound. A famous
violinist once pointed out that a violin string is of no value
lying loose on a table. It is only when the string is put on
the violin, bound, and properly tuned that it is free for the
first time to sing. This is also true for us. When we decide
on values, goals, and our purpose in life and allow ourselves to be bound to them, we become attuned to life and
truly feel a sense of liberty and freedom.

THE WORD IS
Life

Every time I look at the sea I get the same feeling. The great expanse of water, stretching to touch the distant horizon, speaks of mystery, adventure, and risks to be taken. The waves curl and break on the sand—teasing, beckoning, whispering, and laughing. And such is life. You have a life to be lived. Live it with joy and a feeling of awe. If you read or study, let your conclusion be: "I have a life to be lived. What can I do? What can I learn that will help me to live a life that beckons me to new horizons?"

THE WORD IS
Light

Albert Schweitzer once wrote, "The one essential thing is that we strive to have light in ourselves." From his writings we can assume that his definition of light included our searching for knowledge, developing wisdom, and allowing the inner light that is in all of us to shine through. He explained that "our strivings will be recognized by others and when people have light in themselves, it will shine out from them." It is implied that even the striving for light will help us and may touch the lives of many. So when it is dark, do not curse the darkness. Just remember to light a candle.

THE WORD IS
Listen

If you want to be interesting *to* others, be interested *in* them. Begin with the next person who speaks to you. Give him your full attention. The good listener is so rare these days as to be completely fascinating to people. Most of us greet friends with "How are you?" but we never find out because we are just waiting to tell how *we* are. And it's no fun to talk with someone whose eyes and thoughts are obviously wandering. Recently I read a poster inscribed, "Listening is a way of loving." It is a good thought to remember. Listening *is* a way of loving!

THE WORD IS
Longing

Longing is the hunger of the heart. When you feel it, you are being reminded that the inner you is still growing and needs new experiences and ideas as the body needs food. Longing is not a feeling to be suffered, but a feeling to be welcomed. If you never longed for anything life would be dull and you yourself would be static. You would stop growing. Longing keeps you moving, seeking, growing. So don't wish you didn't feel longings; find ways to fulfill them. It has been well said: "The pangs of longing are the forerunners of achievement."

THE WORD IS
Love

We can all agree that we need love in our lives and that the world needs love. The reason we find it difficult to establish a permanent value to live by is that no definition encompasses it fully. Love may be expressed as kindness, concern, regard, or caring. It may even come disguised by gruffness or anxiety. But we all have a basic instinct to love and we feel better for expressing it. We need not define it. To express love is to enrich your life and the lives of many others.

THE WORD IS
Material

If you want to build something, anything at all, you begin to gather the tools and materials with which to build it. With all that has been written or said about "positive thinking" it continues to be the hardiest tool we possess to build a better quality of life. Learn to watch your thinking. How do you start the day? How do you view a situation in your life? What kind of thoughts make you most unhappy? It seems almost too simple to be true, but it is true. Thought by thought we can form the habit of thinking positively and build what we want out of the right material.

THE WORD IS
Maturity

It is doubtful that any of us can reach full maturity in a lifetime, but at least we can know something about what to
look for. Developing a strong physical body, getting an
education, filling a job may only represent the tip of the
iceberg. A part of maturity is learning to wait patiently
when it is necessary. We must accept change as inevitable
and not become disoriented by it. We must understand
that our intuition and feelings are often a better guide than
our thoughts. Increasing trust in yourself as a person, maintaining poise and serenity in any situation should assure
you that you are moving toward maturity.

THE WORD IS
Meaning

Anyone who practices the art of pantomime knows that he
must become highly skilled in projecting meaning and feeling to others without the use of language. Every facial expression, every move, every gesture becomes highly important. There may be something in this that applies to all
of life. Often misunderstanding arises when we fail to con-
vey to others what we really feel. To live in harmony with
others is to focus all of our faculties on projecting the right
meaning in the right way.

THE WORD IS
Meditation

You know, meditation can be a time of pleasure and renewal, and often is of tremendous help. However, when many people hear the word meditation, they think of a Far Eastern master sitting in a lotus position in disciplined concentration. But in its simplest form, meditation is a time when we go alone, when we still the body and remove all the busyness from the mind. In quiet contemplation you will find strength and inspiration and often, if you listen, you will find the assurance that all things are working together for your good.

THE WORD IS
Mirth

The laughter of a little child is musical and infectious because it is so filled with mirth. It is a genuine feeling of joy and lightheartedness. We may often laugh without feeling mirth. We make sounds that are supposed to be laughter, but may carry a note of sadness, or even apprehension. True mirth has been described as "laughter with a smile." If you've lost the ability to feel mirthful, try to recapture it. It has a healing power.

80

THE WORD IS
Money

A great part of our life is spent in giving thought to matters of a financial nature. A better job with more income, the right investments, how to spend less and save more, and on and on it goes. There is nothing wrong with this except that so many of us are disappointed with what we get compared to what we want. We need to have concise, explicit knowledge of what money will buy and what it will not buy. Satisfaction, freedom, joy, and a sense of wholeness are not for sale. Each of us must find out how they are attained and then pay the price.

THE WORD IS
Moods

Can you control your moods, or do your moods control you? It may be helpful to be fully conscious of our moods moving in cycles. It is easy to see cycles in natural forces, but more difficult to be aware of such cycles in ourselves. If on any given day you are depressed, anxious, or insecure, try to remind yourself that it is simply a mood. This mood may be the result of a natural cycle. However, you have the choice of whether you control moods or moods control you.

THE WORD IS
Motivation

Self-motivation is probably one of the most difficult qualities to achieve. We may know of some new project we would really like to take on. We may have good intentions and even a strong desire, but procrastination is a formidable foe. Often we must plunge right into whatever we want to accomplish. We may make a few mistakes or find it necessary to revise our plans, but motivation requires action, and by taking action we escape the trap of "I'll do it tomorrow."

THE WORD IS
Mystery

Mystery is a word that has many different meanings, but at this moment let's think of the mystery of life itself. In spite of the great advances of science, there is much about each individual that is a mystery to others, and even to himself. We ask the questions, "Who am I? What am I? What am I here for, and where am I going?" The complete answers to these questions seem to remain a mystery. We discover many things about ourselves, but never is the discovery full and complete. But as long as we keep in mind that we are on the way to solving the mystery, we will not stand still or stagnate.

THE WORD IS
Need

Whether it be modesty or a feeling of unworthiness, you
may have a tendency not to believe in yourself as much as
you should. This very attitude may prevent you from ac-
complishing some of your most cherished goals. Learn to
affirm yourself. In times of quietness literally talk yourself
into greater self-confidence. Say, "I am real. I am a person.
I have thoughts and feelings and desires. The world has
need of me and it is my full intention to fulfill that need!"

THE WORD IS
New

With the coming of spring there is a dramatic, almost mystical sense of newness in all living things. We can almost feel in the very air this sense of new life as plants, trees, and flowers begin to show their lavish beauty. We are not just onlookers in this feeling of newness, or at least we do not need to be. New courage and optimism come to us as we identify with nature and understand that new forces of life move through us as well as through other living things, and we can experience the spring of renewal in our own mind.

THE WORD IS
Nourishment

We give much thought and time to an intake of food that will serve as nourishment for the physical body. However, there may be times when your whole being needs nourishment. Doing your work, relating to people, a day of any kind of activity may require that you expend much energy. Even a night's sleep does not always replenish or give nourishment to your mind and emotions, as well as your body. Getting back to nature, a time of quietness, finding a sense of serenity all may be sources of nourishment for the soul.

THE WORD IS
Now

Nothing so affects our overall feeling of happiness and well-being as learning that the important time is now! Seneca said, "One should count each day a separate life." This is a difficult art to master. It is so easy for the mind to turn backward with regret or forward with apprehension and neither adds anything to living a fulfilling life now. The time of now is so filled with possibility, challenge, and opportunity that we have no need for yesterday or tomorrow.

THE WORD IS
Obedience

You may not like the thought of obedience if it implies to you a kind of subservience to some source of authority that you may not fully trust, but let's look at it from another viewpoint. We may spend half a life looking for greater wisdom, light, and insight, but fail to act according to that insight after it is found. How many times have you heard someone exclaim, "If I had only followed my hunch, things would be better." Actually, he might be saying, "I sought guidance and received it, but failed to act with obedience."

THE WORD IS
Objective

We are told to be objective, to know what's going on around us, and to face the reality of the world outside ourselves. This is sound advice only when we understand that there is a reality inside us that is just as real. Our inner world consists of our thoughts, our feelings, our memories, and promptings from our intuition. A person who is really in charge of his life moves back and forth between these two worlds with ease and confidence, and neither the inner nor the outer is neglected.

THE WORD IS
Observe

Henry Thoreau's genius was due in part to his highly developed power of observation. He could make a dramatic episode out of a squirrel crossing from one tree to another. Try this mental exercise: Look around you and observe that which is within range of your vision. Then see how many different ways you can describe what you see. Practice this exercise at least once a day. It probably won't make you a Henry Thoreau, but it is sure to increase your enjoyment of life and you will be amazed at how much is going on around you that has passed by unnoticed.

THE WORD IS
Offer

One of the quickest ways to rid ourselves of vague, unpleasant feelings that are going on inside us is to go out and do something constructive for someone else. You may have had the experience of offering to help someone and being rebuffed, but at least you made the offer. We all see situations daily where we know we could be of real service to another but are hesitant to make the offer—and later have feelings of regret. There is a real sense of joy in knowing that others think of you as a person who wants to be helpful.

THE WORD IS
Open

One of the most rewarding actions we can take is to strive to be more open with ourselves and our feelings. If you are annoyed, angry, impatient, or depressed, trying to hide such feelings is the surest way to mishandle them. Wouldn't it be wonderful if employer and employee, friend and friend, husband and wife, parent and child, could trust each other enough to openly express themselves? Even if we must tread lightly with others, we can be open and honest with ourselves and what we truly feel.

THE WORD IS
Opportunity

A vivid illustration of how we limit ourselves by accepting some weak cliché is contained in the statement, "Opportunity only knocks once." One must ask, "Opportunity for what?" Sure, we can all remember times in our lives when the wrong decision seemed to cause us to pass up a golden opportunity. But what about the dozens of opportunities that come knocking at our door every day? The opportunities to cultivate a deeper feeling for life, add a cheerful note to a dreary situation, encourage the discouraged. They knock all right, but we must open the door.

THE WORD IS
Optimistic

The person who is steadily optimistic knows exactly what he is optimistic about. It has nothing to do with government, politics, or the state of our economy. It begins with the person who is willing to accept himself and others while knowing that improvement is needed and will probably come. When a person believes that improvement is not possible, he is already in the midst of complete pessimism. No matter what goes on around you, if you continue to work toward improvement, you will remain optimistic and you can be sure that better things will come.

THE WORD IS
Order

Begin now to affirm that you are calm and poised and all things will work together in an orderly manner. There will be time to mail cards, buy gifts, and plan the celebration of a great event. Somehow there will be sufficient funds to meet your needs. Any special season becomes difficult if we allow ourselves to feel rushed, disorderly, and tense. The best guarantee against this is to formulate the attitude that all things are in order. Remain calm and proceed in an orderly manner to do whatever you need to do.

THE WORD IS
Organization

Everyone finds it necessary from time to time to organize himself in order to keep growing and moving toward his objectives. Organization of our inner life is a lifetime process, but it should not be thought of as a dreary, unending struggle. There is great satisfaction in using discipline and persistence in lining up our thoughts, feelings, desires, and actions and moving in an organized manner toward our highest goals.

THE WORD IS
Original

In the life process no one knows when he is being really original. Without being aware of it, he may be borrowing his idea from someone else. This may not be so important, since anyone with a good idea likes to see it used. It is important, however, to think of new and original ways of solving our own difficulties when they arise. Every person experiences times when he feels like saying, "I have tried everything that I know, and nothing works. I am about ready to give up." It is at this moment that concentrated thought on original solutions becomes invaluable.

THE WORD IS
Others

We all know that we live in two worlds: the world outside and the world inside. When faced with a life situation that is difficult, or an inner feeling of unpleasant anxiety, these must be met within the realm of our own consciousness. However, such feelings or situations may begin to yield in the simple act of doing something helpful for another person. What we do may be totally unrelated to our own problem, but positive, helpful action sets into motion our powers and faculties for overcoming.

THE WORD IS
Participation

Life in these times may have a tendency to push people toward being spectators rather than participants. You may read about what others are doing or watch television shows of interesting people doing interesting things until you feel left out and settle for just watching. You may even become convinced that there is not much in which you can participate, but if you settle for that, you may live only half a life. It may be fun to be a spectator, but it is much more fulfilling to find that in which you can participate.

THE WORD IS
Past

It is not so important to try to keep the mind from turning to the past, but it is extremely important to learn how to handle what the memory digs up. We have all had times when we said or did the wrong thing at the wrong time. We may have committed acts of weakness and we may have hurt ourselves or others. If you have such thoughts, you have lots of company. The fact is, you probably did the best you could with what you had at the time. Remember, the hard experience can sometimes be a better teacher than the life of ease.

THE WORD IS
Patience

Patience is the great preventer. It prevents hasty, ill-advised words and actions. It prevents panic when things don't seem to go right. It also prevents pessimism, even when others around us are pessimistic. A recent news article stated that there is much pessimism among the people in America. We should remember that we live in a great country and its greatness lies in the people who live in it. No one knows all the answers to our national problems, but with work, optimism, and patience, the answers will come.

THE WORD IS
Peace

When we think of trying to achieve peace of mind, we may feel that this can only come when the mind is completely free of fear and anxiety. It is necessary for us to realize fully that states of mind are relative. While scarcely anyone is ever completely free of fear and anxiety, it is possible to let such states grow until they are out of all proportion to any real threat. Face your fears. Often they are impostors. Tolerate your anxieties; trust and they will become less intense. It is thus that peace of mind is created.

THE WORD IS
Perception

In order to establish a meaningful relationship with another person, you must be able to perceive what he is really like. This means that you not only hear what he says, but you perceive and understand what he is feeling. It is also quite probable that you may have a deep longing for someone else to perceive and understand you in this way. This kind of relationship is one of the most treasured things in life—or should be. Take any person in your life circle, perceive him as he really is and try to understand him. You may be amazed at what happens.

THE WORD IS
Perfection

Perfection is an elusive goal, mainly because no one knows what it really is. Many think of a perfectionist as being one who is highly skilled, who demands the best from himself and others—and usually gets it. The psychological definition is a little different. A perfectionist invariably demands *more* of any given situation than the situation itself calls for. Consequently, he lives in the land of "never enough." He may find it difficult to function at all. Content yourself with what is good and you will behold improvement coming to meet you.

THE WORD IS
Persistence

We give much attention to the value of inspired and creative thinking. However, when real inspiration comes to us, our work is only half done. We are called upon to work hard with a kind of patient stubbornness until we prove whether or not the idea has merit. If you are inspired about something you want to do, be prepared to carry through. The world might still be using candles for light if Edison and others had only said, "I think an incandescent lamp might work."

THE WORD IS
Personal

Have you ever had anyone start to tell you something and then preface the statement with "Now I don't want to be personal"? Personal is a good word. It speaks of knowing one's self as a person and being willing to become involved with other persons. Those who do a good job of what they are doing do it because it has a personal meaning for them. They have a deep desire to pursue something to its completion. No sooner do they make a discovery than they have an urgent desire to share it with another person. The need is not to be less personal but to dare to be more personal.

THE WORD IS
Pleasure

None of us want to waste our lives in a constant search for pleasure, but some experiences that bring pleasure are healthy and stimulating. We all have built-in pleasure-pain reactors. When painful tension turns into relaxation of mind and body, we feel a deep sense of pleasure. A visit with a friend, a walk through a place of natural beauty, listening to music, whatever brings you enjoyment and wholesome delight are a part of creative living. A life that includes pleasurable experiences is a life that is worth living!

THE WORD IS
Poise

The word poise brings many pictures to mind. I usually think of the poised person as one who never gets rattled, never panics, continues to think clearly in the midst of confusion, and radiates a strong feeling of self-assurance. Few of us have attained all this but would probably like to. If we do, it means that we have been able to build into our consciousness strong feelings of strength and confidence. We then would become more like the person Emerson described, "Who in the midst of the crowd, keeps with perfect sweetness the independence of solitude."

THE WORD IS
Positive

Many people are turned off at the mere mention of positive thinking. Their interpretation is that you are trying to make a rose out of a cabbagehead by just thinking it will happen. Such is not the case. Learning what positive thinking is can often work wonders. Learn to hear yourself when facing some difficult situation. If you are saying, "I don't think I can do it. I don't have the ability or the energy," that is what positive thinking is *not*. "I think I can. I'm going to try. I believe I'll make it." *That* kind of thinking makes the difference.

THE WORD IS
Preparation

So often our reaction to any life experience depends on how we prepare. When we think of preparing for busy times—buying presents, social engagements, or other unusual demands made on us at a special time of year—we may think that getting it all done early is the answer. We may also forget the kind of preparation that should receive first consideration; it has to do with inner preparation. We need to set up a series of constant reminders to do what we have to do with poise and confidence and refuse to let anything disturb us.

THE WORD IS
Price

We can enter any retail store and find objects that have a tag on them giving the regular price and then a sale price that is much less. However, there is much that is worthwhile in life that never goes on sale. If you have some cherished goal that you know is worthwhile, it is quite possible that you may attain it, but you have to pay the full price. That price often demands concentration, decisions, and self-discipline. Before you give up on any goal, ask yourself if you are really willing to pay the price.

THE WORD IS
Quality

In what was called the "energy crisis," we saw people reacting in various ways. Some tried to hedge against it by storing up products that were in short supply. Others were ready to push the panic button and exclaim "All is lost." Still others spent too much time trying to decide who was to blame. But there is another way. It consists of looking for the good that may become manifest. Let's stop measuring the good life by the quantity of our possessions and look toward a quality of life based on positive values and convictions.

THE WORD IS
Quietness

When there is something we want to do or need to do, we usually think in terms of action. We must think harder, work harder, move faster, take action! There is a season for action, but sometimes we need a time of quiet, when we are not acting at all and the mind is still as well as the body. At such times we are receptive to new ideas. We also replenish our energy and find new strength with which to work. In a moment of serene quietness, you may find the guidance you need to point your action in the right direction.

THE WORD IS
Reflection

When we pause to reflect on our lives, we may become conscious of qualities we once had but now have lost. Innocence, youthful exuberant enthusiasm, and many more may come to mind. It is then we need to remember that life is a process. Some things simply cannot be held onto. In their place, however, there may come a deeper appreciation of life, and a greater awareness of what is true and lasting and beautiful. Let your reflection fill your heart with gratitude for what you have now!

THE WORD IS
Relating

Forming a good relationship with another is dependent on leaving him free to become what he wishes to become. We know he is in the process of painting his life portrait and since he has not yet finished we aren't called upon to criticize his efforts. While it is true that we can never paint another's life portrait for him, we may sometimes be in a position to hand him a brush. If this is the attitude we would like from others, we should be able to relate to them in the same way.

THE WORD IS
Release

It is amazing how at times we can free ourselves of some mental or emotional burden by simply releasing it and letting it go. You can't afford to live each day with building resentment. It is like some toxic element accumulating in the system, which causes disease. You may feel that your resentment is justified, but even if it is—*if* you keep repeating it continually to yourself and others, you are the one it hurts, not the person or circumstance you are resenting. Release it, let it go—forget it!

THE WORD IS
Repair

Any time our relations with others seem to be breaking down, this is very good evidence that they are in need of repair. This is not so difficult as it might at first seem. Whether it be our family, friends, or someone who is just trying to be helpful, a few words of appreciation, writing a note, remembering to be thoughtful and courteous can cause our human relations to improve dramatically. When people who are meaningful to us seem to become more distant, we need to take up our kit of tools and make some repairs. It's better still to keep such relationships in good condition by nurturing them as we would any precious possession.

THE WORD IS
Repose

The one who barges through life in a constant hurry does not necessarily cover the most distance. We need time to reevaluate our direction and efforts. There must be times when, in complete rest and relaxation, we sit back to enjoy the accomplishment of the day. Longfellow put it this way:

> Each morning sees some task begun,
> Each evening sees it close,
> Something attempted, something done,
> Has earned a night's repose.

103

THE WORD IS
Resourceful

The best way to maintain a sense of fulfillment that is free from frustration is to be resourceful. This involves the ability to look around, see new possibilities, and move toward their accomplishment. Many, many people have been discouraged by the fact that when they pass a certain age, no employment is available to them. This does not happen if we continue to cultivate our resourcefulness. If we have developed several skills, we open new doors when old doors are closed. We all have untapped resources to call upon in time of need.

THE WORD IS
Rest

Adequate rest is a must in everyday living and involves more than just sleeping a prescribed number of hours at night. Every day offers several opportunities, even though they may be only a few minutes, for rest and relaxation. To take full advantage of such times we need to remind ourselves that we can be physically inactive, but if our thoughts are not harmonious, we are still using energy. Some people feel guilty when they try to rest, thinking of a dozen things they should be doing. Learn to sit quietly, and say to yourself, "Nothing in this world bothers me." You will find that your energy is soon replenished.

THE WORD IS
Revelation

In these times it is easy to observe a new wave of pessimism, doubt, and discouragement with each new report of national or international news. What a wonderful revelation it is when one finally knows without question that one is in charge of ones life. With this there comes the complete assurance that one can live through these changing times and meet any difficulty in the knowledge that it does not have to control or destroy one. Seek diligently for this revelation, for it is the source of peace and serenity.

THE WORD IS
Season

In nature, winter varies with the physical location on the earth. At times, winter brings the beauty of icy branches, clean white snow, and skaters gliding gracefully over frozen lakes. What one feels at any given time makes winter bleak or beautiful. We are not called upon to live through a long winter of discontent. By setting our own moods, we make our own seasons, and biting winter winds can be made to give way to joy, warmth, and inspiring contemplation.

THE WORD IS
Security

There are many sources of security. If you are in a plane, it is the pilot. In a car, it is the driver. Some think money is a source of security. One source of real security is always to use our ability and energy in productive ways. At any time in life, regardless of our age, *if* we are using the creative potential we have, we are creating situations that bring security. One who finds this inner security finds it more durable than anything outside himself. Real security is the knowledge that you can face and successfully work through any situation life brings.

THE WORD IS
Seed

In his book, *As a Man Thinketh*, James Allen writes: "Good thoughts and actions can never produce bad results. This is but saying that nothing can come from corn but corn; nothing from nettles but nettles. Men understand this law in the natural world and work with it; but few understand it in the mental world."

By your thoughts and the actions that spring from them, you are constantly planting seeds; and you must harvest the resulting crop in your life. Sow the seeds of confidence, kindness, industry, goodwill, and generosity and the harvest will be these same things.

THE WORD IS
Selection

The power of selection in our thinking does not mean that we select only certain facts about life and ignore all others. It more accurately refers to our being highly selective about the factors that mold our attitudes and influence our life in general. We can become discouraged when attempting to digest current events unless we learn to select that which is encouraging and give it priority. Even in the face of great challenges, we have the right to select attitudes that will keep our vision and courage strong.

THE WORD IS
Self

Somewhere along the line we must come to an acceptance of our own selves. This means developing an objective recognition of one's abilities and limitations, virtues, and faults. It means freedom from undue pride or self-blame. It is not something passive, but leads one to constructive efforts. Self-acceptance means a healthy approach to life.

THE WORD IS
Selfish

This is one of the words in our language that needs to be reviewed. We tend to brand selfishness as bad and unselfishness as good. We must remember that we are human beings and one of our basic needs is to speak and act in ways that make us feel good about ourselves. Some of the world's finest accomplishments have come about because someone understood the principle of self-investment. When we do something for others that we know is right and good, we are making an investment. No one is branded as totally selfish who does good for others in order to feel right about himself.

THE WORD IS
Self-Sufficient

We spend most of our lives believing that our happiness depends on some person, some situation, or the attainment of some material objective. It's little wonder that we find it difficult to believe that the most important step we can take is to become self-sufficient. There is an inner strength and guidance that moves us toward real security, peace, and joy and we must search for this center of our being and find it. We then find that our relations with others, our goals, and our actual achievements are enhanced by this feeling of being self-sufficient.

THE WORD IS
Sensitive

Whether being sensitive is constructive or destructive depends on the direction this sensitivity is allowed to take. To be sensitive to our own true feelings about others helps us to understand our own lives better and deepens our relationships with others. To be overly sensitive to criticism or to the actions of others towards us is another matter. It can cause us to wear our feelings on our sleeves or withdraw through fear of being hurt. You are the one who controls the direction your sensitivity will take.

THE WORD IS
Serenity

When we see a person who has an unusually high degree of serenity, we may feel that he has not had to meet many serious problems in life. A closer look tells us the exact opposite. A serene person is usually one who has met many difficulties in life but somehow has learned to meet them in the right way. Attaining serenity is not easy. If your goal is to remove from your life all that disturbs you, that goal may never be reached. Serenity comes only through learning to trust life and to trust your ability to meet any life situation, knowing that you are moving toward the highest and best for you.

THE WORD IS
Serious

Living is serious business and many things must be taken quite seriously; but how often do you find yourself taking something far too seriously? Your serious thought may be out of all proportion to the situation, and may cause you anxiety and undue worry. Try to lighten your load. Remember to laugh and take lightly that which should be taken lightly. Your chances for taking life too seriously are far greater than for not taking it seriously enough.

THE WORD IS
Share

As we share our thoughts and feelings with others, it is not difficult to observe that what we send out comes back. Kindness begets kindness. The attempt to understand another, prompts him to try to understand us. The desire to help calls forth that same desire from others. If, through some feeling of negativism, we express quick irritation, anger, or intolerance, we may well expect others to react the same way. We make it much easier on ourselves when we try to share only our very best!

THE WORD IS
Sight

It is a literal fact that we may have perfectly healthy eyes, but fail to see. Take the time to look around you and see how many things you have allowed to go unnoticed. The most common object can become a thing of beauty when studied in detail, while we are thinking of all the component parts that went into its creation. There is nothing wrong with dreaming of faraway, beautiful places, but when we have a highly developed sense of sight we can look up and see a thousand wonders of the world right where we are.

THE WORD IS
Silence

Have you ever walked through the woods in some remote place, when no breeze rustled the leaves, no sound came from near or far? If you have, you will know what is meant by the indescribable experience of silence. Some fear silence, others make no effort to seek it, but it is a part of our wholeness. This is especially true when you are trying to get in touch with yourself and the rest of the universe. In the words of the poet, "Silence alone is great enough to hold a thing so real it never can be told."

THE WORD IS
Simplicity

Have you ever known someone who can take the simplest of problems and complicate it beyond description? Opposite to this is the one who takes a problem that seems most complex and simplifies it until it can be fully understood by almost everyone. There is a premium on this quality of simplicity. It is a complex world in which we live and those who help to simplify it help everyone. Tolstoi said, "There is no greatness where there is no simplicity, goodness, and truth."

THE WORD IS
Spiral

Try to think of your life as a spiral going higher with every turn. Whatever happens in your life gives you additional experience in handling any life situation. You may have difficult experiences, but they can be a time of learning, enabling you to move on to better things. When you merely go around in circles, you tend to meet the same problems over and over; but gaining the concept of your life as a spiral will help you to understand that you can move onward and upward to better things.

THE WORD IS
Spring

Not all of human life follows the pattern of nature but there is often a similarity. Springtime is often blustery and windy. The memory of winter is still fresh in your mind and the renewed life of spring is not yet too visible. Yet you know it will come. Have you ever felt that you had reached a dormant period in your life when nothing seemed to be moving forward? At such times it is good to remember that spring will come, with new hope, new vision, and new ideas pushing for expression. The most beautiful season of all is when springtime comes to the human heart.

THE WORD IS
Stability

So much is said in these times about the value of being ready and able to change or to accept change that it might be well to give some thought to the counterbalance. It is true that changes are coming so rapidly in our world that it is startling, which is a very good reason for developing the quality of stability. Even in the midst of progress, a time must be taken to consolidate your position. To be a stable person in no sense implies that your life has become crystallized.

THE WORD IS
Stand

It seems pretty safe to say that everyone has anxieties with which he must wrestle. Some of the anxieties are justified and some are not, but it doesn't alter your feelings. The difficulty lies in the fact that quite often you can't even identify the source of your anxiety and fear. The poet put it this way:

> The thing that numbs the heart is this: Man
> cannot devise some scheme of life to banish
> fear that lurks in most men's eyes.

One thing is certain, however; when you stand firm, trust your highest self, and face your anxieties, you can handle them much better.

THE WORD IS
Step

One seed makes a tree and many trees make a forest. The addition of one drop of water at a time turns a stream into a river; the river flows to replenish the sea. One step at a time is the way we make our journey through life. As we think of what lies ahead, we can find relief from tension by realizing that we're not called upon to live a whole year in one day. Our highest aspirations are reached by taking one step at a time.

THE WORD IS
Stimulation

Much has been said about boredom being the disease of our age, and it is true that many are bored with their jobs, bored with other people, and perhaps bored with life itself. So we ask, "If we are bored, what is the antidote?" The answer is stimulation, and this must come from within. The easiest way to stimulate the flow is to be aware of a continuing learning process. To learn something new every day is the surest way of finding healthy stimulation. Boredom cannot remain.

THE WORD IS
Strength

Everyone is subject to periods when he wishes his life could be easier. Yet we all know that we grow through meeting difficult situations in the right way. Just as physical muscles grow stronger through use, the whole person becomes stronger through accepting a challenge and working to overcome it. There are those who bemoan the high degree of frustration caused by the difficulties they encounter. Others seem to enjoy taking up the challenge. Anyone can find strength if he views life as a growing experience and is not afraid to take up the challenge.

THE WORD IS
Suggestion

You may have heard someone refer to the "mere" power of suggestion, but suggestion is not mere. It is a real power, whether we are using autosuggestion or receiving the suggestions of others. Our attitudes towards our work, family, friends, and life if general are often formed by the power of suggestion. This power can become a great strength or a detriment, depending upon the kinds of suggestions we allow our minds to dwell on. Try starting every day with the positive suggestion that you are strong, capable, and confident. You will find that it does make a difference!

THE WORD IS
Tendency

When we think in a certain way for long enough, we form a tendency to think and react to life within the framework of what we have made habitual. Such is the case with irrational guilt. If you are carrying an unnecessary burden of guilt, get rid of it! Any person who is constantly on the defensive, or does not do well in his relations with other people, may well be ruled by guilt feelings. If this is true of you, change the tendency, unload the burden, and feel the freedom and joy to which you are entitled.

THE WORD IS
Think

When we consider the process of education, most of us would readily admit that we were taught many things, but that there was very little emphasis on *how* to think. This is especially true when we want to think in an original manner. Here is a simple process, which may be helpful to you. Choose something you are interested in and begin to concentrate on it. Your first thoughts will probably not be very original. Concentrate some more. Let it rest for awhile and then come back to it. The influence of other people's thinking will begin to fade and original ideas will come. No one has a corner on original thinking.

THE WORD IS
Thinking

Anyone who constantly thinks negatively will also have negative feelings. But this process can be reversed. We often try to let the tail wag the dog by saying, "I cannot think positively because I don't feel that way." Thought patterns can be changed through persistence. Grief, resentment, anxiety, or anger are human feelings, but should not be allowed to remain too long. Start now to think positively. Picture yourself as a person who feels good and thinks positively. To think right is eventually to feel right.

THE WORD IS
Tides

For all of us life has tides that ebb and flow. When the tide runs strong, there is a sense of fulfillment and success. When the tide ebbs, it does not mean that the sea of life has deserted you. It should be a time for listening, a time for rest and renewal, a time for reviewing your present situation and deciding what you really want to accomplish. Strong tides will come again, and on the rising waves of faith and hope you will be prepared for positive action.

THE WORD IS
Time

Time seems to rule our lives. We never have enough of it. It slips away before things can be completed. One little boy said he liked his grandmother because she didn't have a watch. Obviously, this observation was based on watching people scurrying around him, from one thing to another, always worried about time. Time truly can be a tyrant. But time is for us to use, we cannot let it rule our very existence.

THE WORD IS
Tolerance

It is difficult to have feelings of tolerance for people we don't understand. While, to a certain extent, we all have similar needs, no two paths of life are identical. Before we judge someone for being the way he is, we should try to understand how he became that way. The person who is most often misunderstood is the one who has the deepest need for love, friendship, and someone who will express an interest in him. Learning to express greater tolerance toward each other is the first step in building harmonious human relations.

THE WORD IS
Trust

Are you worried about the actions of another person today? Do you wish you could nudge that person this way or that, just for his own good?

You know, our intentions may be fine, but if we nudge, we are trying to live someone else's life for him. It just can't be done. There is only one way to help another person and that's by trusting him to live his own life. Trust awakens the best in others and helps them make good decisions. Those who are trusted are encouraged and made wise. Those who trust find peace of mind.

THE WORD IS
Values

It is easily observable that the people who get the most out of life are those who are able to laugh, to love, to be humorous, to fantasize, and to enjoy uplifting emotional experiences. Whatever else we do, these qualities can add much to our lives, and the best part of it is that they can be learned or relearned. Sometimes we let things slip away from us because we don't place a high value on them. Deadly serious times are no more important than those of lighthearted enjoyment.

THE WORD IS
Viewpoint

It is helpful to remember that what we call failure has only as much restricting power as we choose to give it. When we attempt something and fail, either in the eyes of others or in our own eyes, we may waste too much time looking for the cause. We can neutralize the experience faster if we remember similar situations in which we were successful. It all depends on our viewpoint. We can compound our problem by rehearsing it, feeling sorry for ourselves, and giving up; or we can resolve it by remembering that failure is overcome if we view new possibilities for success.

THE WORD IS
Vision

We all need the vision necessary to see our lives in the right perspective. From the moment we are born, our life begins to change and continues to change as long as we live. He who sets out to fight that change swims against a current that is too strong for him. We all have the ability to lift our vision to see new values, new goals, and to form new attitudes. This is one of the tools we work with in letting go of the old, accepting the new, and putting ourselves in harmony with the natural growing process.

THE WORD IS
Volition

Volition carries the meaning that one has the power of choosing or determining the direction of any given life situation. The wise person does not spend his time in conjuring up all the areas in which he does not have a choice, but concentrates on situations where he has. We have volition, or the power of choice over our thoughts, feelings, attitudes, and actions, which means we can determine the direction of our lives. To move constantly toward the best life has to offer, we need to exercise our volition with decisiveness and determination.

THE WORD IS
Wait

One positive sign of maturity is knowing how to wait.
Something may arise for which there is no immediate
answer. Intellectualizing about it does not help. One man,
who was meeting a crisis in his life, stood in his rather ex-
tensive library and exclaimed with anguish, "There is
nothing between the covers of all these books that can give
me an answer. I will just have to wait and know." Some
situations yield to positive action; others require that we
calmly and trustingly wait.

THE WORD IS
Wisdom

The journey through life is not always easy, and our paths are by no means clear. Every life experience carries the potential for a valuable lesson, but we need to understand it, and that requires wisdom. Knowledge is not always synonymous with widsom. Even a little child can express an idea that is profoundly wise. There are no set rules for finding wisdom, but the desire to seek it out and express it is the first step on the journey.

THE WORD IS
Yourself

We often consider the importance of cultivating friend-ships with others, but it is just as important to learn how to be a good friend to yourself. Learn to live with yourself. If you dislike other people, it may indicate that you dislike yourself. No one is perfect, and everyone has quirks. The chances are that you are doing a pretty good job of living your life. You will never have to worry about having friends if you use your intelligence and common sense in making yourself your best friend.

THE WORD IS
Zest

To live with a zest for life it is necessary to work with a fundamental principle: "The world outside us can only be improved by expanding the world inside us." This need not be a heavy, boring process. The truly zestful person learns to look for every sign of personal progress in his feelings, attitudes, and reactions and is ready to exclaim, "This is great! I am making progress. I am understanding myself better. I feel better about life and my life is getting better." You can never get bored with life if you learn to enjoy the slightest sign of progress.